A CREATIVITY WORKBOOK

FOR PHOTOGRAPHERS

First published in 2020 by Emma Davies.

ISBN: 978-0-9956324-4-8

EmmaDaviesPhotography.com

Contents

"OUR DOUBTS ARE TRAITORS AND CAUSE US TO MISS THE GOOD WE OFT MIGHT WIN, BY FEARING TO ATTEMPT."

William Shakespeare, Measure for Measure

About Emma

Emma Davies has both Bachelor's and Master's degrees in Psychology with a special interest in teaching creativity. She has been a photographer since 2005 and a photography instructor since 2014. Before her photography career she was a lawyer practising in London.

Emma's flagship beginner's photography course is called **A Year With My Camera**.
She is also the author of **Beginner's Landscape Photography**. You can find links to buy these titles at AYearWithMyCamera.com.

She teaches beginner and intermediate courses online. For more details visit emmadavies.photo/courses.

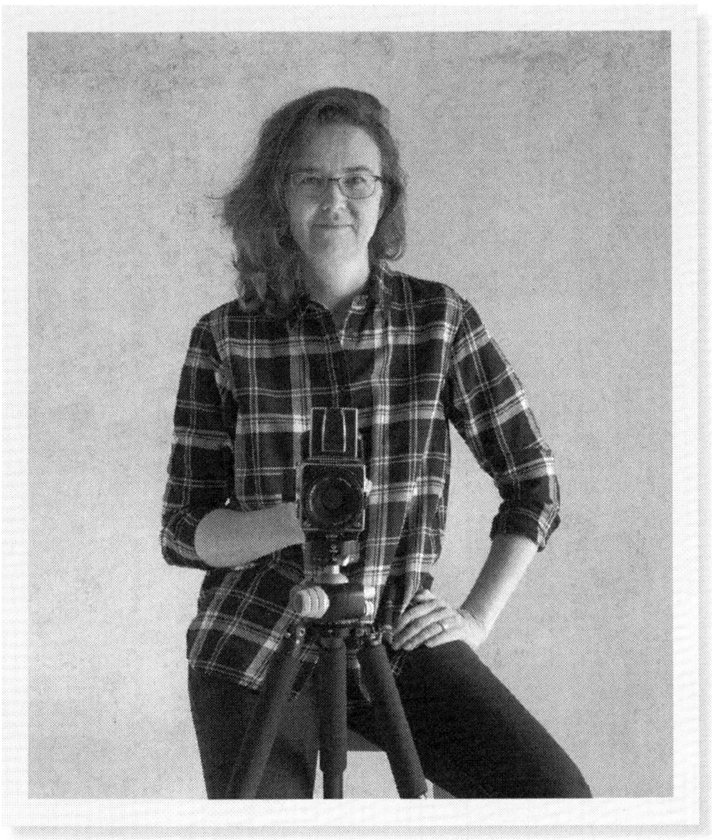

How to use this book

THIS BOOK ISN'T HERE TO TEACH YOU CREATIVITY. IT'S GOING TO HELP YOU REDISCOVER THE CREATIVITY THAT'S BEEN THERE ALL ALONG.

The book is designed to be written in. Underline things that you want to remember. Scribble in the margins. Fill in the boxes. Doodle in the blank space. When you get to the end of it, it should look completely different to anyone else's workbook.

Forget everything you learnt in school. In this book:

- there is no right answer
- there is no wrong answer
- nobody will tell you what you should do
- you won't be marked out of ten
- you can do the same exercise on two different days and get two different results

CHAPTER 1

What is creativity?

CREATIVITY ISN'T DEFINED BY SUCCESS. IT ISN'T BEING ABLE TO PAINT THE CEILING OF THE SISTINE CHAPEL, COMPOSE THE MOONLIGHT SONATA OR WRITE THE HARRY POTTER SERIES. IT'S NOT EXCLUSIVE TO WORLD-FAMOUS PHOTOGRAPHERS SUCH AS ANSEL ADAMS, HENRI CARTIER BRESSON OR DIANE ARBUS.

Creativity is simply the ability to make something from nothing. It's the ability to start with only your thoughts and then let them out into the world in whatever form you want – it could be painting or writing, cooking or coding.

Art is just one expression of creativity. But if you've ever looked at what you have in your cupboard and made a meal with that instead of following a recipe you have been just as creative as someone who makes a sculpture or draws a sketch.

Creativity is part of being human. The need to move beyond the status quo, to be curious, to follow a train of thought, to see what happens if we put this with that, to express an emotion with brush or pen or camera – this is what makes us different from computers.

Why are you reading this book? What do you hope it will help you with? Write your thoughts below:

Whatever your end goal remember that creative photography is achieved when you make something that is unique to you. It doesn't have to be a completely new style of photograph or an image nobody has made before. Nobody else has lived your life, seen the things you've seen, daydreamed your daydreams. Your brain is waiting right now to cook up some new ideas, make new connections, suggest new photographs: all you need to do is give it the right conditions to get to work.

The process of creative photography is made up of:

- your mindset: your motivation, confidence and "get-up-and-go"
- your cognitive skills: your ability to make new connections, draw on your experience and generate ideas
- your practical skills: your ability to use your camera to its full potential

This book will help you achieve the right mindset for creative photography and will show you how to optimise your cognitive skills. If you need help with practical camera skills, take Emma's beginner's course, *A Year With My Camera* (details at AYearWithMyCamera.com).

Am I creative?

Do you consider yourself creative? Mark on this scale where you think you are, creatively:

not at all creative									I couldn't be more creative
1	2	3	4	5	6	7	8	9	10
○	○	○	○	○	○	○	○	○	○

If you give a five-year-old a pencil, a piece of paper and no other instructions they will start drawing or making marks. If *you* were given a pencil and a piece of paper, what would you do with them?

What happens between being five and being twenty-five or fifty? Where does that unbridled enthusiasm and lack of inhibitions go?

George Land did some research in the 1960s that involved testing the creativity of the same children at the ages of five, ten and fifteen. He also gave the same test of creativity to a cohort of adults.

The five year olds scored ninety-eight percent.
The ten year olds scored thirty percent.
The fifteen year olds scored twelve percent.
The adults scored an astounding two percent.

The good news is that the creative five-year-old inside every one of us is still there. We may have learnt to be less creative through the way our schools work, the expectations to conform and the pressures of adult responsibilities, but we can also unlearn this and let the five-year-old out again.

Learning creativity as an adult is essentially one long unlearning process: you will be unlearning rules, assumptions and habits that have built up over the years. It will be uncomfortable at times but ultimately liberating.

The most effective way to make progress is by doing – not by reading or listening. That's what this workbook is for: to show you how to peel away the inhibitions you've built up since you were a child and allow your innate creativity to have a voice again.

DRAWING: WHERE THE INHIBITIONS STARTED

When you were a small child with a pencil in your hand you just drew. You drew mostly out of your imagination. It didn't matter if it was realistic. You didn't care. The adults around you didn't care. You were praised simply for drawing.

At some point, usually around eight or nine years old, you became aware that some people were really good at drawing. They could look at a tree and draw a realistic picture of that tree. They could sketch a landscape or illustrate a bird beautifully. You looked at your own drawings and decided they weren't any good. Nothing had changed in you. You were still the same person who was praised aged three for doing the same thing.

A small minority of people at this stage seek out drawing teachers. They ignore the critics (both themselves and other people) and work hard to make the transition from naive mark-making to being "someone who can draw". It doesn't just happen. They have to practise.

But if drawing and art weren't a priority in your family or school when you were a child then it's unlikely you were helped through this transition. You probably put down your pencils and mentally consigned yourself to the bucket of "people who can't draw". And because drawing is so closely related in our minds to creativity you might, at the same time, have labelled yourself, consciously or subconsciously, "not creative".

TRY THIS

Take five or ten minutes now and draw these eight items in the space provided. Four are common items and four are made-up items. Notice if you find either set easier and/or more enjoyable.

a bird	a zagger
a house	a mumflump
a tree	a smeefly
a bicycle	a tractoid

THREE STAGES OF CREATIVITY

Researchers of the creative process agree there are at least three distinct stages to any creative endeavour:

- information gathering
- incubation
- output

The first and last stages are conscious acts, involving effort and action on your part. The incubation stage (where you let your subconscious do the work and make new connections) is passive, but you can actively create optimum conditions for this stage.

The model of creativity that involved these three distinct stages was first cited in the 1920s by Graham Wallas. The idea of "stages" of creativity was groundbreaking at this time. Previously it was assumed you had to be a genius to be creative, that creative insight arrived in a single "Eureka!" moment and that creativity was a gift from the muses. The relatively new science of psychology (born as an independent discipline in the 1870s) gave scientists the tools and methodology to study the human brain and ultimately build and test theories of the cognitive origins of the creative process.

Since the 1920s many models of creativity have been proposed but the one thing they all have in common is the idea of these separate stages, each adding something critical to the process. If you omit the information gathering stage you will keep repeating what you already know. With no incubation stage you deny your brain the opportunity to make new connections. And with no output stage all you have is daydreaming.

The rest of this section of the book gives an overview of the three stages of creativity. All of the exercises in the following chapters have been designed to help you make progress in each of these three stages: information gathering, incubation and output. Don't forget there is no "right" way to be creative. Work with an open mind even if you think an exercise is pointless or doesn't apply to you. You are allowing all the ideas to percolate with the goal of enabling your unique expression of creativity.

INFORMATION GATHERING

You have been gathering information your whole life. Every book you've read, every film you've watched, every conversation you've had – they have all added their mite to what is your life experience. To become more creative as a photographer you simply have to take a more active, conscious approach to your information gathering instead of passively consuming out of habit.

How does this affect you, practically? Before you start on a particular project, you should take the time to gather inspiration and outline your goals. And, in general, try to become more open to new experiences.

In Chapter 5 you will find detailed exercises to help you identify new, helpful and inspiring influences. At this beginning stage however, you just need to be aware that curiosity goes hand-in-hand with creativity. At school or work you may have been encouraged to narrow your focus, to become an expert in one small area. Now you have permission to read, watch, consume anything you want to. The more diverse the better.

Openness

Wenfu Li (a professor of psychology in the USA) has demonstrated that being willing to encounter new situations or information – basically being curious about things – is one of the main predictors of a higher degree of creativity in an individual. And the good news for us all is that this "openness to new experiences" is not a character trait you have to be born with. We can all actively get out of our comfort zones, try new things, go to different places and meet new people.

INCUBATION

Incubation is the stage where you simply mull over your ideas. You have been curious, read around a subject, gathered inspiration – now you need to let your brain digest all this input. Give it the right environment for incubation and your brain will take the new information, add it to your life's experiences and start to make new connections. You may be aware of this happening, you may not be. You might have a "Eureka!" moment or you might just find yourself drawn to take photographs of a particular subject or in a particular style.

The "right environment" is being in a state of relaxed awareness. You are not watching TV or running a personal best. You are not cooking a complicated meal or helping children with homework. You are doing something slightly engaging that doesn't need active thought: walking, driving, showering. This state of relaxed awareness is covered in more detail in Chapter 3.

If you've followed my work for any time you may have heard this story: when I had the idea to start a free, online photography workshop for complete beginners the main thing I wanted was to be the opposite of all those courses that promise you can learn photography in a weekend – because you can't. I didn't know at that stage what structure my workshop would take, what order the lessons would be in, or exactly how I would differentiate myself in the very crowded online photography course market.

I had spend weeks researching the competition, talking to students I already taught, doing lesson plans, drawing out ideas (the preparation stage). Then (to my slight annoyance) Christmas got in the way. I had to curb my enthusiasm, put all my notes away and focus on the celebrations. And – of course – I had my "Eureka!" moment when I was half way through peeling a mountain of Brussels sprouts. Vegetable prep is perfect for incubation: slightly engaging (or you'll cut yourself) but repetitive so it doesn't need any decision-making. The name "A Year With My Camera" just popped into my head, fully formed. I wasn't even thinking about the course – I wasn't thinking about anything. I put down my paring knife, registered AYearWithMyCamera.com at 4pm on Christmas Eve, then got back to the kitchen to finish the pile.

You can't force this stage. Preparation and output are conscious, active, directed stages. During incubation you just have to let go and trust your subconscious to start making neural connections that will present as a new idea. Sometimes it will and sometimes it won't. It helps to be in an optimistic frame of mind otherwise you can easily shut your subconscious down with thoughts like;

"I'm not creative"
"I never have good ideas"
"This is pointless"
"This is taking too long"

Instead, prepare your subconscious for success with thoughts like;

"The ideas are in there just waiting to come out"
"I trust myself"
"This is fun - who knows what might happen"
"I have a lot of creative energy"

TRY THIS

Pick one of these positive thoughts and write it down, and stick it somewhere you will see it every day.

OUTPUT

At some stage you just have to start taking photographs. You've researched the light, the settings, the subject and the inspiration. You may be overwhelmed with different ideas or you may think you have none. You've taken some time – five minutes or five months – to incubate your ideas. Now you just have to make a start.

There's no correct time to start but the more you repeat the cycle of preparation, incubation, output, the more you come to recognise when you are good to go.

In Chapter 7 you will learn many techniques to overcome common blocks that stop us from picking up the camera and starting the output stage. Be aware that your first shots will not be your most creative ones. You need to trust your subconscious and just give it the freedom to express itself as you go forth with your camera.

Photographing in a group

Think carefully (and honestly) about how you react to being in a group. Many people enjoy the energy that comes from working with others. But I think many more people, even if they won't admit it, don't do their most creative work in a group setting. You have to be able to manage the distractions that arise in a group which affect your ability to sink into your own mind and indulge yourself. You need to make compromises. These aren't optimum conditions for individual creativity.

If this sounds very selfish it's because being creative is a selfish endeavour. You are making time for your own personal development to the exclusion of everything else. It doesn't mean you will never again photograph with friends – it just means that the aims of the day will be different. In Chapter 8 you will learn how to find creativity in collaborative work but this collaboration is a very specific situation where all parties are committed to a joint creative output rather than a photo walk with friends where everyone has different priorities.

CHAPTER 2

About me at the beginning

WHO ARE YOU? WHERE ARE YOU ON YOUR CREATIVE JOURNEY? TAKE SOME TIME TO PUT SOME MARKERS DOWN AND EXPLORE WHAT MAKES YOU, YOU.

My earliest memory of playing.

My earliest memory of being creative, of producing something new to me.

Was creativity rewarded when I was a child? Give an example.

Did anyone ever tell me I couldn't sing or couldn't draw or couldn't write?
If so, who? How did I feel?

Who encouraged me to experiment artistically?

How old was I when I realised adults valued realistic drawings more than enthusiastic scribbles?

When did I last have fun?

What am I afraid of when I pick up my camera?

What do people say I'm good at?

What do I think I'm good at?

When did I last sit and do nothing without looking at my phone for more than five minutes?

Who do I most admire and why?

What could I easily teach someone else how to do?

What did I want to be when I was a child?

What do I want to achieve by picking up this book?

What am I nervous about right now?

MY INFLUENCES

What are my "desert island discs" (the six songs I would choose if I were stranded on a desert island)?

Which three books would I gift to my children or someone close of the next generation?

What do I love that other people find weird?

If I could visit any single piece of art in the world right now, what would it be?

CHAPTER 3

Making space

CREATIVITY IS *NOT* A DIVINE GIFT; IT NEEDS A DEGREE OF HARD WORK AND APPLICATION. AS WITH ANY ENDEAVOUR YOU WILL NEED TO MAKE SPACE FOR IT IN YOUR LIFE.

SCHEDULING

Getting started is one of the biggest hurdles. So just make a start. Do the next section in this workbook every Sunday evening or Monday morning until you have finished the book. No interruptions. It is said that people find money for the things they really want - the same is true of time. You find time for the things that matter to you. If you consistently fail to find time for photography and creative development - is it really that important to you?

How much time can you realistically set aside to work on your creativity, and for how long can you keep this up? Imagine this workbook as a single term (semester) taking ten weeks to complete. Can you set aside an hour a week? A whole morning? One day each weekend? More? Block out the time in your diary now and honour it as if you were expected to show up in a classroom.

WRITE IT DOWN

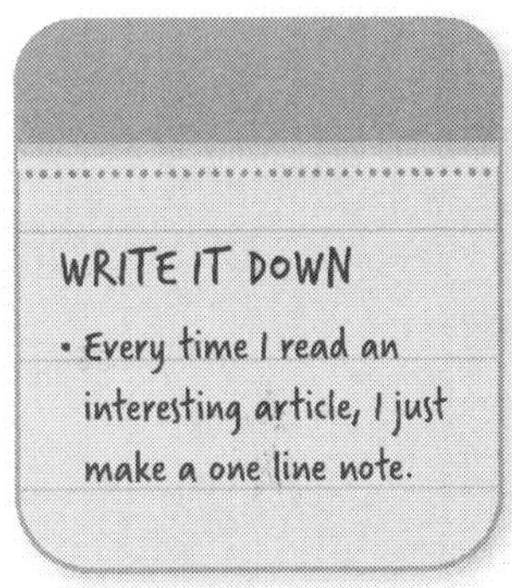

You need to have a quick and easy place to capture the ideas that will come to you at all times of day and night. I use the Notes app on my phone. In fact I wrote the entire outline of this workbook over about a year in my Notes app. Every time I read an interesting article, was reminded of something I learnt during my Master's degree or came across some new research I just made a one-line note. Over time I had pages and pages of notes and when I came to sit down and write the book all I had to do was arrange them into categories and then work on the detail.

Whatever you pick has to be frictionless, i.e. it needs no effort on your part to record the idea. If you have to find your favourite pen or open up a document on your laptop each time something occurs to you it is unlikely you'll actually write it down.

OPTIMISE YOUR ENVIRONMENT

There is a balance between becoming so obsessive about arranging the ideal environment that you never get started, and working in situations that are filled with unhelpful distractions.

There are a few things you can do to your physical and emotional environment to optimise your chances of creative breakthroughs without becoming so reliant on them that you can only work in one single ideal setting.

1. Get rid of things that don't serve you as far as you can.
This includes expectations, clutter, unsupportive people, unrealistic to-do lists and distractions. But recognise that your environment is never going to be perfect; get used to making a start in less-than-ideal circumstances.

2. Move more.
Many studies have shown that sitting still all day decreases creativity. There may be more than one reason why:

A. Sitting still is not conducive to having a "clear head". Simple walking clears the head and allows the brain to make connections and solve problems. A Stanford University study from 2014 showed that a person's creative output increased by sixty percent whilst walking (indoors or outdoors). The study does not show exactly how walking has this effect but they suggest walking might be the first step in a causal chain that ends in physiological changes in the brain. The good news for people who can't walk is that similar effects may be found in "the mind-freeing quality of engaging in a comfortable task" – knitting for example.

B. Exercise has been shown to help create more proteins called brain-derived neurotrophic factor ("BDNF"). These proteins actively drive cognitive growth, stimulating the creation of the new neural networks that are essential for creative thought.

C. Reduce stress. Whilst you can be creative whatever your mood, too much stress suppresses creativity because being creative takes energy: actual oxygen and glucose, used by the brain to make new neural connections. If you are stressed (physically or mentally) your body uses up oxygen and glucose quickly and your brain is forced to revert to proven and predictable ideas, making it much harder to take risks and explore new ideas. Note that one paradox of creativity is that a small amount of stress can be helpful. People who are completely calm, who have no deadlines or other calls on their time, can be too serene and may find their brain is slow to work.

3. Sleep.
If you don't get enough sleep you will find it hard to concentrate, you won't be able to make decisions or learn new skills, your coordination will deteriorate and your creativity will plummet. You need a good night's sleep to recover physically and mentally.

Of particular interest to creatives is the rapid eye movement ("REM") stage of sleep which mostly occurs in the last third of a normal night's sleep. During this phase the chemical make-up of the brain is altered allowing changes to occur between neural connections. New ideas are formed whilst we are unconscious. Out-of-date ideas are dropped. Although this all happens while you are asleep the effects carry over into the next day and you will find you are more creative when you are getting enough REM sleep than if you are running a deficit.

4. Nutrition.
Is it possible that what you eat can affect how creative you are? Evidence is building that it can; there are more and more studies showing there is a relationship between your gut health and your cognitive processes. Even at an anecdotal level we can all relate to that heavy, slow feeling we get after a big lunch, or the way we can't concentrate on anything when we are very hungry, or how even a slight degree of dehydration can significantly reduce brain function.

Studies have shown that eating more fruits and vegetables correlates to more curiosity and creativity. This may be because participants ate less sugar as they increased their fruit and veg count, or it may be because they were moving to a naturally less inflammatory diet which increases blood flow to the brain.

Keep your own food diary. Write down what you eat every day for a month and also keep a note of how curious, creative and motivated you feel, each on a scale of one to ten. Try and keep other aspects of your life constant (amount of sleep, amount of exercise). Does eating less processed food make a difference? What about keeping well hydrated, cutting down on alcohol or eating less sugary food? If you eat a lot of bread and pasta do you notice a dip in energy afterwards?

DOING NOTHING

When were you last alone with your thoughts? When have you recently had ten minutes with nothing to do but wait: no book to read, no companion to talk to, no phone to amuse you? The age of the smartphone is undoubtedly a great advance for humankind but the way it leaves us "always on" is having a detrimental effect on our capacity for original thought and creative insight.

"Incubation" is a necessary stage for the creative mind. At some point you need to stop what you are doing, put down the distractions and simply sit with your thoughts. Twenty or thirty years ago we could do this at a train station or as a passenger on a long car journey, when you'd finished your library book and had nothing to do but stare out of the window. But now the smartphone is always with us, full of ways to keep us busy in what would have previously been productive downtime.

What happens if you never get bored? Your brain is always consciously doing something. It never has a chance to let the new inputs and inspirations settle and to hook up with existing neural networks to create new connections. When you are properly bored your brain enters something neuroscientists call "default mode". This daydreaming state of mind means you are not responding to the world, you are not creating thoughts as a response to something happening; instead you are experiencing true, personal thoughts, generated from within.

Next time you are waiting for someone or something with nothing else to do, instead of reaching for your phone simply sit and wait. Follow your thoughts. See where your attention goes.

Being bored is a privilege. Reframe boredom not as something to be feared but as an opportunity, a gift of time to let your brain fire its neurons and lay down new neurological pathways. Being bored is uncomfortable, but a bit of discomfort is good for us – it's an opportunity to *create* our way out of the boring situation. It's difficult to do the first few times but I promise you it gets easier. Don't give in to your brain which will be screaming at you to pull your phone out for a quick distraction. Sit it out and see what happens.

TRY THIS

Step one: put your phone away and find a pen.

Step two: just sit and be for half an hour. Daydream your heart out. If the boredom gets unbearable, start doodling. Use this space. Carry on over the page whenever you need to.

What direction did your mind take? Set aside some time to do this activity for fifteen minutes at least once a week. Keep notes afterwards about whether you drift into negative, guilty thoughts (remembering old grievances or thinking about all the laundry you haven't done) or positive, hopeful thoughts (remembering good times or planning for the future). Try and nudge your thoughts into positive channels or let them simply come and go.

If you have a particular creative problem you want to solve you can write it down at the start of your boredom session. You might not come up with a solution during that session but your brain will have the opportunity to store the problem and to start making new connections. Your subconscious will go to work and ideas will pop up at unexpected times in the future once you have laid the ground work.

NOTES

CHAPTER 4

The rules

WHAT ARE THE RULES OF CREATIVITY?

The rules of creativity we learnt*, and were rewarded for following, as children were:

- Colour inside the lines.
- A drawing should look like the thing you are drawing.
- Neatness is the goal.
- An adult will give us a set of instructions to follow carefully.
- Do it right or don't do it at all.
- Hurry up and finish.

These rules have left us with a sense that:

- Taking risks is dangerous and results in disapproval.
- Having fun not the aim.
- Someone else will tell us what to do; we don't need to think for ourselves.

* I think in the last 10 years there has been a shift in priorities within schools and there is a move towards recognising more freedom of expression for children. Hopefully when the current generation grows up they won't need books like this one and they won't need to unlearn inhibitions.

What happens if you break these childhood rules?

- You start to think for yourself.
- Creative doors that have been closed to you start to open up.
- Your brain has permission to come up with ideas that don't follow the rules.
- You start to have fun once again.

It's harder work but the rewards are greater

- It's not risk-free: taking risks and living with the consequences is part of the journey.
- You are responsible for motivating yourself.
- You are free to follow rabbit-holes and pursue spontaneity but you will necessarily step off the safe conveyor belt taking you from here to there.

BREAK THE RULES

The photography world is steeped in rules, conventions and maxims. Many are hangovers from days of shooting film (the recommendation to use a UV filter, for example), others are designed to mark out advanced photographers as the ones who know what they're doing ("sharpness at all costs"), and others are promoted by camera manufacturers to minimise user error ("don't shoot into the sun").

If someone tells you that you "should" or "should not" do something, ask them, "Why?" until you are satisfied with their reply. People often don't make it past the third "Why?":

"You should shoot on manual mode."
"Why?"
"Because that's what proper photographers do."
"Why?"
"Because it makes better photographs."
"Why?"
"I don't know..."

TRY THIS

Take these photographs, all of which break a photography "rule".

- [ ] The shot is deliberately out of focus.

Stick photo here

☐ No clear subject.

Stick photo here

☐ Shoot at midday in bright, harsh light.

Stick photo here

☐ Put the horizon in the middle of the frame.

Stick photo here

Don't forget: nobody remembers how sharp your shot was. They only remember how it made them feel.

TAKE RISKS

Creative people do not settle for the status quo. They do not simply keep doing what is already working. They acknowledge "the rules" but know the rules don't suit every circumstance. They have new ideas. Some ideas will be successful, others won't. But nobody knows which is which until they try them.

Risk-taking gets easier with practice. The first time you do it you will be very nervous. The self-preservation part of your brain will be doing all it can to make you to stop – it wants you to err on the side of *not* taking the risk because you don't know what will happen. You have to work through this resistance to become an accomplished creative risk-taker.

I'm not asking you to take risks where lives are at stake. The worst that will happen is that you take a photograph that doesn't work.

As you work through this book take the opportunity to try things where you're not sure what will happen. Embrace failure. If every photograph you take is perfect then you are not taking enough risks. Aim to fail. Fail often. Reframe the way you take photographs so that you *expect* to make mistakes – if you're not making mistakes you're not making progress.

You can do all this risk taking and failure in private. You don't need to show anyone your photographs. But you do need to make a pact with yourself to review your images as dispassionately as you can and give yourself objective feedback.

You don't learn from your easy, perfect shots. You learn from making mistakes and actively working out how to fix them.

TRY THIS

Keep a list of the creative risks you take whilst you are working through this book. Write down anything you try where you didn't know whether the image would be successful before you pressed the shutter. Aim to fill these pages by the time you finish the book.

RISKS I HAVE TAKEN

RISKS I HAVE TAKEN

JOURNEY OVER DESTINATION

Take a moment to consider this scenario: the next time you go out with your camera you take a shot so amazing, so perfect, that you know you can never take a better one. You have "arrived". Everyone who will see the photograph will be overawed. It will go on to win competitions and be sold around the world.

What happens next? How do you get up the next day? What would be the point of going out with your camera?

Having goals can be a good thing with photography. Goals give you something to work towards and help with motivation on off-days. But pick your goals carefully. I would advise against aiming to "arrive" or "finish".

Our childhoods were punctuated with tests and examinations. In many cases we learnt a topic, passed an exam and were told we had finished that topic. History springs to mind as an example in my case. I learnt little pockets of historical fact (the causes and effects of the First World War, the expansion of the American frontier in the 1800s), took an exam to prove I had memorised the salient facts, and I never revisited those facts again.

This routine of learn – test – finish stays with us for the rest of our lives. It's not surprising that when we start to learn photography we think there is a finish line to cross and once we cross it we will "be a photographer".

Photographers lose out creatively by rushing towards this imaginary finish line. *There is no line*. Photographers who expect some arbitrary validation once they "finish" are doomed to disappointment. You will always have something new to learn, another style to try, another muse to inspire.

If we do away with the "hurry up and finish" feeling that drives almost every aspect of twenty-first century life, what are we left with? What side-alleys will be able to explore, which whims will we have time to indulge?

If you imagine your life with your camera as a journey rather than a destination you can slow down and enjoy the moment you are in. You will have learnt the secret to fulfilment that most photographers never know. You can – dare I say it – have fun.

TRY THIS

Draw two sketch maps.

Map 1: the "sprint to the finish" journey with your camera. Decide on one goal (it might be winning a competition, selling a photo, getting your LRPS). Mark off and label all the steps you need to take between now and finishing. Include deadlines for each step. This is akin to using the "SMART" goal productivity technique (having goals that are specific, measurable, attainable, realistic and time-bound).

Map 2: the "journey over destination" adventure with your camera. There are no rules for this one. Map out one example of what a fun and fulfilling lifetime of photography might look like.

Both of these maps have their place in your photography journey. If you want to earn a qualification or win a competition you will need to focus on that goal for a time to the exclusion of all else. But for the purposes of leading a creative life with your camera then the second option will be the one to embrace. It is riskier, a bit unsettling and people following a more traditional route might look down on you. But never forget this is *your* life and *your* creative adventure.

CHAPTER 5

Habits

THINK BACK TO THE FIRST THIRTY MINUTES AFTER YOU GOT OUT OF BED TODAY. HOW MANY DECISIONS DID YOU MAKE? HOW MUCH WAS ON AUTOPILOT? CLEANING YOUR TEETH, CHECKING YOUR PHONE, MAKING COFFEE, UNLOADING THE DISHWASHER, WAKING OTHER PEOPLE UP. NONE OF THESE THINGS NEED A CONSCIOUS DECISION – WE JUST DO THEM.

Habits are efficient. If we had to make a decision about every single thing we did each day we would get very little done. Fortunately the brain loves to work on autopilot. Getting out of bed is a trigger to clean your teeth or otherwise start the day the same way as you did yesterday. Once you've driven the same way to work a few times you no longer need to think about the route.

At a neurological level what happens is this: a triggering action occurs (getting out of bed, getting into the car) and the brain fires up the neurons it has used every day in the same situation to prompt the next action using minimal mental energy:

GET OUT OF BED > CLEAN YOUR TEETH

GET INTO THE CAR > DRIVE TO WORK

Habits are great for productivity but bad for creativity. Your brain will want you to take the easy route because it uses less energy. In photography terms this translates to the following habits:

- You reach for your favourite lens.
- You shoot on an aperture you are comfortable with.
- You visit places you are familiar with.
- You work at the same time of day.
- You have a routine you are happy with.

Keep doing the same things and you will keep getting the same results. To be more creative, to spark new ideas, you will need to break out of the cycles of automatic responses and habits you have become accustomed to. It will take effort and practice. Often, drastic action is needed to stop the brain taking the easy route. And, like many steps on the way to a more creative life, it will be uncomfortable to start with.

You don't need to spend your entire life from now on avoiding habitual behaviour but an awareness that a particular action *is* an automatic response is needed to prompt creativity from time to time.

AWARENESS OF HABITS

Awareness of habits is the critical step. If you know you are doing something out of habit (driving to work, for example) you can decide if that's OK or if you'd rather have some active input into an action that has gradually become something you do on autopilot.

TRY THIS

Think back to yesterday or any typical day in your life. Think through everything you did. What did you do out of habit? And how many things were truly not done on autopilot? How often did you actually stop, think, consider alternatives and make a decision?

Habits	Active decisions

Now imagine you are going out with your camera for a typical shoot outside the home. Picture the shoot from the moment you start packing your bag to the moment you get home and download your shots. Think of all the actions you make and mark on the scales on the next page whether these are usually made completely on autopilot, whether you make conscious, deliberate choices, or whether they are somewhere in between:

Autopilot —— Careful thought

Where to go

1 2 3 4 5 6 7 8 9 10

When to go

1 2 3 4 5 6 7 8 9 10

Which gear to take

1 2 3 4 5 6 7 8 9 10

What things to shoot

1 2 3 4 5 6 7 8 9 10

What settings to use

1 2 3 4 5 6 7 8 9 10

Which composition to use

1 2 3 4 5 6 7 8 9 10

Which viewpoint to use

1 2 3 4 5 6 7 8 9 10

How to light your subject

1 2 3 4 5 6 7 8 9 10

How long to stay out

1 2 3 4 5 6 7 8 9 10

What post-processing to do

1 2 3 4 5 6 7 8 9 10

Where to share the final shots

1 2 3 4 5 6 7 8 9 10

Now you have a degree of awareness about how much of your life – creative and otherwise – is lived on autopilot you can choose when to step out of the habit and take back control. If you notice you always shoot at f2.8 for the blurred background you might take an extra minute to weigh up the pros and cons of using a different aperture. If you run through the same three or four quick edits on every shot you might pick a couple of shots to work up in a different way.

As I said in the previous section, habits are essential to avoid mental overload. You don't want to end up exhausted from debating the minutiae of every decision. But having an *awareness* of when you are on autopilot means you can spot when you might be missing an opportunity to be more creative.

BREAKING HABITS

TRY THIS

Spend a day doing small, usually habitual things, differently:

- Hold your coffee cup in the other hand.
- Take a different route to work.
- If you wear rings, put one on the other hand.
- Use a different coloured pen.
- Use a different internet browser.
- Sit in a different place when you eat or watch TV.
- Say "yes" to something you'd normally say "no" to.
- Wear something you haven't worn for months.
- Listen to a different radio station.
- Read the news from a source you normally ignore.
- Work standing up.
- Eat lunch at a different time.

ATTENTION

Running on autopilot all day keeps you safer and makes you more productive. But it also means you miss a lot. If you've done A Year With My Camera you'll remember the creativity exercise about really paying attention - the one with the "count the basketball throws" video. (If you missed that one, go to YouTube now and search for *"Daniel Simons selective attention test"*. Don't search in Google because the search results will have spoilers – go directly to YouTube to search. The video is a short, excellent demonstration of the importance of attention).

Inattentional blindness is the term given to the way we sense the world around us without actually noticing it. Without checking, write down the titles and authors of as many books on the closest bookshelf to you as you can. No bookshelf? Write down all the news stories from today including reporters names:

To become a more creative person you will need to stop living life superficially. Stop cruising through the day looking but not actually seeing. Now and then you need to stop and *really* pay attention.

The good news is that it is easy to overcome inattentional blindness. All you need to do is direct your attention. Be an active participant in the world rather than drifting through. Remind yourself to notice things, to be curious.

TRY THIS

The fork

- Sit with a fork for five entire minutes – no distractions, set a timer.
- Draw the fork in as much detail as you can manage in the space below.
- Once you've drawn it, start taking photographs of the fork.

TRY THIS

Three photographs

- Visit a new place or, if you can't get out, set up a new shot at home.
- You are only permitted three photographs for the whole duration of the shoot so you'll need to think first. Explore all your options, consider the light, debate different settings and contemplate alternative compositions before you commit to the three photos.

TRY THIS

Take a daily photo for thirty days

Aim for a reasonable goal. It might be simply to take a thoughtful shot on your phone or to take a photograph at the same time every day. Once you have committed to the project, see it through. It's only thirty days. Don't miss a day – tick them off below. Pay attention to how your motivation comes and goes and how easy it is to find a photograph you want to take.

1	2	3	4	5	6	7
8	9	10 How is my motivation?	11	12	13	14
15	16	17	18	19	20 How is my motivation?	21
22	23	24	25	26	27	28
29	30					

KEEP THE GOOD HABITS

Habits aren't all bad. One way you can turn a habit into a good creative tool is by embracing the discipline it can bring you. Musicians practice daily for a reason: they want to embed muscle memory and become proficient. Writers will write daily because otherwise their book will never be written. There is always something else more appealing to do than sit down and do the work.

One practice you can adopt as a photographer is taking a daily photo for a period of time. Some days it will be easy, other days you will not want to make the effort. But the routine of picking up your camera and looking for a shot primes your brain that this is expected behaviour and it becomes easier – habitual – over time.

Many people choose to do a "Project 365", or take a photo every day for a year. Whilst I applaud the ambition I think this is actually too big an ask. You risk becoming utterly disheartened and resenting your camera. Start with thirty days. A month is a manageable timeframe. You will reap the neurological benefits of the trigger-response reaction resulting from an embedded habit (pick up your camera and look for a shot) but you won't become stale.

WHO DO YOU SPEND TIME WITH?

Entrepreneur and motivational speaker, Jim Rohn is often quoted as saying that you (and your ideas) are the average of the five people you spend the most time with. This is an easy idea to visualise but I think it's a bit simplistic.

At the beginning of this workbook I suggested that your creative output is determined by many things, including, at the preparation stage, your social influences. I do believe that the people you surround yourself with (in real life or virtually) – whether there are five or fifty – will shape your creative output. For example, if the only photographers you talk to are obsessed with sensor size and sharp lenses, then this becomes your "normal".

When I started doing landscape photography I thought the only legitimate expression of the genre was a carefully composed big vista, sharp from foreground to horizon, shot at sunrise or sunset. Why? Because that was the only landscape photography I saw. People I followed on Instagram, my early instructors, outdoor photography magazines: they all had this narrow – albeit spectacular – idea of what the ideal landscape photograph was.

When, later in my outdoor photography journey, I stumbled across the sub-genres of intimate landscape photography and black and white landscape photography I felt nothing but relief (and some annoyance that I'd spent a couple of years battling to adopt a style of photography that wasn't mine).

We are all in the habit of keeping our social circle the same because it's uncomplicated that way. It's easier to go out for an evening with people we know than with a group of strangers. It's less challenging to follow the same kinds of people on social media than to move out of our bubble.

I'm not telling you to ditch your friends and family and only talk to strangers. But, like everything in this chapter, an awareness of your habits will help you move outside your comfort zone occasionally. New social influences will mix up your creative inputs and could result in something different at the output stage.

TRY THIS

- [ ] Find a way to meet people who you feel are more creative than you and who you aspire to be like. This will shift your perception of what's normal and expand your comfort zone. You can do this through in-person events you find on sites like CreativeMornings.com or MeetUp.com. Or, to meet virtually, you can dive into whatever social media site is popular right now – it might be Facebook or LinkedIn groups or Instagram hashtags. If you live near a town or city with a museum or cultural centre, look up their community outreach programme. Go along with an open mind. If you expect to meet interesting people you are more likely to find them.
- [ ] Audit who you follow online. If you only follow photographers, find other creatives to follow: poets, printmakers, potters and painters.
- [ ] Pay attention to how much you value the opinions of those closest to you. If you are trying to build up your confidence to try something new, often your nearest and dearest aren't the best people to show your first attempts to. They can be unintentionally discouraging, or superficially positive – usually because they want to protect you by encouraging you not to take risks.

WHAT DO YOU SPEND TIME WITH?

As for our social influences, so for our cultural influences. Are you stuck in a cycle of reading the same kinds of books, watching the same style of TV programmes, listening to similar types of music and only visiting exhibitions you know you'll enjoy?

TRY THIS

For each category below, write down in the first column what would be your preferred style or genre and in the second column write down some things that are very different, that you might find challenging.

	Preferred style	Something different
Book		
TV		
Film		
Music		
Art		

Now commit to consuming at least one thing from the "something different" column for each category before you finish this workbook and tick off when completed.

PHOTOGRAPHY HABITS

TRY THIS

What photography habits do you have? Write them down and do the opposite for a week.

- What is your go-to lens? Put it away for a week, use one you don't like.
- Always shoot aperture priority? Shoot shutter priority.
- Always shoot contre-jour? Shoot with the light full on your subject.
- Are you a landscape photographer? Try portraits.
- Never use your phone? Only shoot with your phone.

	Photography habit	The opposite
☐		
☐		
☐		
☐		
☐		
☐		

CHAPTER 6

Play

WHEN WAS THE LAST TIME YOU DID SOMETHING JUST BECAUSE IT WAS FUN AND FOR NO OTHER REASON? HARDLY ANYONE THINKS THAT PLAY IS BAD, AND YET AS ADULTS WE RARELY PLAY.

Studies have shown that being allowed a period to play prior to being set a creative task results in more creative ideas being generated.

Playing requires conditions that will be familiar to the student of risk-taking creativity: directed attention, not knowing the outcome, curiosity, improvisation and a willingness to do something new. The player is given autonomy to make the rules. These conditions are exactly those that allow the brain to make new connections between neurons and to link ideas. The player is able to step out of a routine, to break free from habits and to have the confidence to go their own way. Playfulness helps you unlock your creativity.

OPEN PLAY

How can we, as adults, recreate the carefree play of our pre-school days? Has anything leapt to mind as you have been reading? If so, put this book down and go and do it.

The most important ingredient from a creative benefit perspective is that you play in an "open" environment rather than a "closed" one.

- Having a new box of Lego and following the instructions meticulously is "closed" play: there is satisfaction in following the rules but no chance to try your own ideas. Having a box of mixed-up Lego and no instructions is "open" play: you are free to build whatever you want.
- Buying an adult colouring book and carefully colouring within the lines is "closed" play: again, there is satisfaction from finishing a page neatly but you are bound by someone else's ideas. Drawing your own design to colour is "open" play.

If you are embarrassed to be seen playing then do it in private. Nobody needs to know.

TRY THIS

Design a game

JK Rowling dreamt up one of the most famous fictional games when she created Quidditch. Design your own game or sport. It can be based entirely in fantasy like Quidditch with its broomsticks and magic balls, or it might be something that could actually be played in your garden using things you find in your kitchen.

Make a bucket list

Compile a "Sixty things to do before I'm sixty" list or a list of places you want to visit or photographs you want to take. Let your imagination run wild. Don't get caught up in practicalities, just make your list.

Play Doh or Lego

If you have Play Doh or Lego in the house – get it out. Have a go. Sculpt something, build something, have some fun.

Build a play fort

Put up an indoor tent made out of sheets, string some fairy lights or build a pillow fort. Change your environment and live in it for an afternoon.

Build a kite

... and fly it.

Play the circles game

Bob McKim designed a game known as the circles game. Draw thirty circles on a blank sheet of paper in six rows of five circles (you can also search online for "Bob McKim 30 circles printable" and print off a template). Set a timer for three minutes and then draw in each circle to turn it into something (e.g. a face). The aim is to fill in as many as possible with the aim of quantity not quality. This exercise helps you generate lots of ideas without self-editing as you go, which is an essential part of the creative process.

MAKE A MESS

"Messy play" is something we thought we'd left behind at nursery school. But it really is liberating. There are no rules and you can't get it wrong. Can you bring yourself to enjoy making a mess?

- Try finger painting.
- Make a Jackson Pollock inspired piece of art (fling paint at paper).
- Just paint: make marks on paper with no planning or thought for consequences.

If you don't have actual paint, how can you innovate? What can you use instead? If you don't want the clearing up to do at the end try using water against the side of the house.

BE ECCENTRIC

"Eccentric" is such a great word for students of creativity. It gives you permission to be extraordinary, to do the unexpected, to be different: all qualities essential to get your creative muscles working well.

TRY THIS

- Draw on something not meant to be drawn on.
- Only photograph very tiny things for a week.
- Draw "my future" using only curved lines.
- Write your CV (résumé) using only emojis.
- Take photos with your eyes shut.
- Make up stories about the people you pass today. Where do they live? Who do they live with? What is their job? Why are they here today? Where are they going? What is their greatest fear? What do they hope for the future?
- Make a pair of shoes out of your junk mail.
- Indulge your curiosity: learn about the Cold War, follow the migration path of the European swallow, study anatomy, take a course in philosophy – whatever sparks your interest.

- In this space write a paragraph about what photography will look like in the year 2050:

- Keep a list of the eccentric activities you try here – make up your own, you don't just need to stick to the list to the left:

Photo play

TRY THIS

- What is the one thing you really want to shoot but think you "shouldn't"? For me it's "collecting" doors – photographing interesting doors I find and creating an image collection. Everyone does it. But why should that stop me doing it? Indulge yourself. Shoot what you really want to.
- See if your camera does in-camera multiple exposures. Most do. Look up how to switch it on and just have a go.
- Try light painting. Use a dark room (or outdoors at night) and the torch function on your phone. Set up your camera on a tripod, or balance it carefully on a chair. Use a shutter speed of about five seconds to start with and use trial and error to work out the best aperture/ISO. Pre-focus manually on where you will be standing. Use the self-timer to fire the shutter, and then take photos where you "paint" with the phone torch.
- Have a go at water splash photography or oil on water with coloured backgrounds (do a quick online search for examples).
- Use a fun filter or app on your phone. Prisma photo editor is a good one to start with.

Keep a note of other ideas you want to try here:

CHAPTER 7

Fear

WHAT IS HOLDING YOU BACK FROM BEING CREATIVE, TRYING SOMETHING NEW AND MOVING BEYOND THE SAFE, PREDICTABLE PHOTOGRAPHY TECHNIQUES YOU USE AT PRESENT?

Imagine you have just been set the task of shooting a series of photographs for a prestigious, public exhibition but in a style that is out of your comfort zone. Perhaps they want abstracts where you usually shoot realistic photography. Maybe they want blurry, out of focus shots where yours are usually razor-sharp. What is your first reaction? Be honest and write down everything you would feel.

Did any of your feelings revolve around fear? Fear of judgment, fear of doing it wrong, fear of being laughed at?

Ever since our first day in school we have learnt to be afraid. We are afraid of being criticised by our peers or our teacher. We are afraid of failing. We are afraid of what other people will think of us. We have learnt to tread carefully if we want to move outside the status quo, to be the "different" one, to swim against the tide. It's much easier to stick to the safe middle ground.

There is no doubt that being creative makes you vulnerable. You are, after all, exposing part of your soul. It takes a thick skin not to care what people say. Yet creative people keep creating. They keep pushing boundaries and putting their work out there. Why? Because they have to. Because creating is part of what makes us human. By suppressing the urge to create we are denying part of our humanity.

> If you suffer from an anxiety disorder or other mental health issue that might be exacerbated by working through this section, seek professional help before trying these exercises.

Start to pay attention when you feel yourself resisting. What are you resisting? And why? A lot of our non-progress comes from automatically agreeing with our subconscious when it tells us not do something or only to do something how we've always done it. The first step in moving off our safe creative plateau is to recognise our subconscious is holding us back. The next step is to acknowledge the resistance and push through it anyway.

PHOTOGRAPHY FEARS

Where do your inhibitions stem from? How have you learnt to be afraid of creating? When (if ever) have you described your life with your camera as joyful, spontaneous, audacious, instinctive or liberated?

I have taught photography since 2014 and, in my experience, students have commonly learnt to be afraid in these familiar situations:

Camera clubs

The idea of camera clubs is a fantastic one: a group of people meeting weekly to chat about photography, compare ideas and learn from guest speakers. If you join the wrong camera club though you can be put off for life. Some clubs have a hierarchy where the "advanced" photographers defend their status in a way that excludes newcomers. "The rules" are ever-present but not articulated. Some members might be threatened by new ideas and they think that giving a critique is a chance to show off everything they know rather than empower the critiqued photographer to improve their photography.

If you have joined this kind of club then please look around and try others, especially if you are at the beginning of your photography journey. I have met too many people crushed by insensitive feedback. Not all clubs are like that. There are plenty of fun, forward-looking, open-minded clubs filled with generous, enthusiastic members. Make sure you join the right one. (To anyone from my own club reading this, rest assured you fall into the second category.)

Facebook groups
There are thousands of photography Facebook groups. Most of them are not moderated. This leads to a *Lord of the Flies* group personality where the "strongest" (the most aggressive, most opinionated, most confident) rise to the top and the "weakest" (those with nuanced opinions, those who are new and those who hesitate to speak up) sink without a trace. The style of photographs deemed acceptable by the small group of "strongest" members becomes the only style anyone dare post. Creativity dies in these conditions as anyone but the stronger members is afraid to post.

Choose your Facebook group carefully. Find one that is moderated and read the aims of the group to see if they align with your goals.

Instagram
Instagram is a great photo sharing site to find and follow inspiring photographers and to share your own progress. I'm writing this in July 2020 and Instagram claims more than a hundred million photographs are uploaded every day. How many of those do you see, and how does Instagram decide what to show you? The algorithm. Instagram learns what kind of photos you like (by recording what you engage with) and shows you more of the same. But it also prefers to show you shots that have already been liked by other people. So eye-catching, over-processed, composite shots of the Milky Way in Patagonia which have already attracted hundreds of likes are more likely to find their way into your feed than equally beautiful but quieter shots of the Sussex coastline.

How does this feed your fears? If you rely on the Instagram algorithm for inspiration you may always be afraid to share your neighbourhood shots for fear of seeming too small, too parochial, too inexperienced.

School
Were you ever told you were bad at art or that you couldn't draw? Or perhaps you were told you couldn't sing? Schools reward academic success and rote learning. Societies want compliant citizens to emerge at sixteen to eighteen years old, ready to be productive and help grow the economy. Creative things like art, drama and daydreaming: these were things you did after you'd done your homework. Undoing the fear of disapproval from teachers (and possibly parents) can take a lifetime.

Technology

Fear of the camera is very common.

- "What do all the buttons and dials do?"
- "If I change something I won't be able to get it back the way it was."
- "I don't understand all the numbers."
- "Why are there so many menus?"
- "My family roll their eyes when I try and use my big camera."
- "I went to a class but the teacher went too fast."

It was to address all these fears that I wrote *A Year With My Camera*. That course works through the camera one button at a time allowing you to learn the ones you need and be able to ignore the rest (all modern cameras are over-engineered and have far too many bells and whistles). You will only overcome the fear of your camera by sitting down and doing the work. *A Year With My Camera* aims to make that as easy as it can possibly be: step by step, one thing at a time (join for free at AYearWithMyCamera.com).

Throughout this section on fears I want you to keep these words in mind: *joyful, spontaneous, audacious, instinctive, liberated.* Write them down. Have them as your screensaver. These are the words I want you to be able to use to describe your life with your camera by the end of this workbook.

1. WHAT'S THE POINT?

One fear that stops us even getting started is the fear that a creative life is pointless, less worthy, or somehow unimportant. This was especially noticeable during the 2020 pandemic when the world was terrified. Who needs artists? What we needed were doctors, biochemists and people who could organise food supply chains. But we are still human. We need to create. We might not need to create all the time and in every situation but don't ignore the call to create just because it doesn't feel like it's the most important thing.

TRY THIS

Write down all the things you think are more important than photography. Include jobs, humanitarian issues or even things on your to-do list:

Now write down all the benefits that come from creative people, including the arts and people who innovate:

This is not a binary argument. I am not saying it's a choice between having surgeons and having sculptors. I am saying that surgeons, sculptors and the rest of humankind will be better at their jobs and more fulfilled if they find a way to express their creativity.

2. IT'S HARD WORK

Author Seth Godin asks those who want to write but can't whether they are in love with the idea of being bad at writing. He asks whether that is part of their identity. I'd ask the same of you. Have you got so used to the idea of being "bad" at photography that you can't see yourself any other way? If this idea has come to define your character then it will be harder to change. Nobody said it would be easy but it can be done if you are prepared for some hard work.

I will never forget one occasion when my kids were small and we had another family over to play. For some reason I was cajoled into playing the piano. At the time I was working towards my performance diploma so I was playing pretty well. At the end of my Bach Prelude and Fugue the other mother said how jealous she was that I could play the piano like that. This comment brought me up short. I wasn't born being able to play. It didn't happen overnight. I'd practised every day for twenty years – up to two, three, even four hours a day. I wanted to ask: was she really jealous of that? Of that hard work? Of all the things she'd need to give up to find the time? Of course I didn't say those things out loud: I just smiled and thanked her for what I think was intended as a compliment.

If you want to overcome any of the fears you face in your creative journey you'll need to put in the hard work, find the grit to keep going and give up other things you might do with your time. You'll need to get up and shoot when you don't feel like it and take hundreds of photos that don't work and that you don't like.

The opposite of fear is not peace. It is courage.

What have you done in your personal or professional life that was hard work? When did you need grit? When did you keep going even though you really didn't want to?

If you've done it once you can do it again. Grit is a transferable skill.

3. FEAR OF EXPECTATIONS

Think back to an occasion when you tried something for the first time, like your first driving lesson. Did your parents, your teacher or you yourself expect you to be an expert on the first go? No. You had the status of a beginner, and expectations were adjusted accordingly.

What about when you had achieved a degree of competency – to continue the driving analogy – the day after you took your "L" plates off? What were the expectations then? Even then you were not presumed to be an expert. Competent and safe? Yes. Expert? No.

The problem with photography is that you lose the "beginner" status very quickly and people expect great things of you, *including yourself*. You can become scared of letting everyone down, *including yourself*.

What would it look like if you gave yourself beginner status again? Or even "competent" status. If you've got off auto mode, know a few things about composition and can read the light – that's great progress but you are still not an expert photographer. At this stage it's like you've taken the "L" plates off and are just setting out on your own on your lifetime journey with your camera.

Be honest with yourself about your skill with your camera and your journey into creativity. Give yourself permission to adjust your expectations to your realistic status. If you have some skill with the technical side of things but have never really paid attention to composition for example, label yourself a beginner at composition and enjoy the lack of expectations and absence of judgment this allows you as you practise.

The following list is my informal index (compiled after years of teaching photography) of where a photographer actually is on the "complete beginner" to "advanced" scale. Because photographers often don't know what they don't know, they often pin themselves as "advanced" as soon as they can shoot off auto. I don't think this is helpful for the rest of their photography career because they often stop learning at this point and lose their curiosity. I haven't published this list to put you off or discourage you. It's here simply to give an impartial guide to help you manage your own expectations of yourself so you can start being kinder to yourself. If you want to create a prize-winning photograph that's great. But you aren't going to pick up your camera and take that winning image the first time you try. *Enjoy* the early stages, the freedom to experiment, the process of making new connections.

Once you can do all these things you are no longer a complete beginner:

- Switch camera on.
- Charge batteries.
- Format memory card.
- Transfer photos to computer.
- Take a photo on factory settings.

Once you can do all these things you are no longer a beginner:

- Switch between manual and auto focus.
- Achieve correct focus.
- Understand what the sensor does.
- Be aware of the exposure triangle.
- Know how aperture affects depth of field.
- Know how shutter speed affects motion blur.
- Know how ISO affects exposure.
- Appreciate some basic composition concepts such as the rule of thirds.
- Know the difference between hard light and soft light.
- Be aware of how light direction affects a photograph.
- Be able to post process RAW files to a basic level.
- Confidently shoot on aperture and shutter priority modes.

Once you can do all these things you are no longer an intermediate photographer and you are on your way to becoming advanced:

- Confidently shoot on manual mode.
- Intuitively utilise exposure compensation.
- Instinctively select appropriate aperture or shutter speed (without conscious thought).
- Easily prioritise compromises (eg. accept a higher ISO for a small aperture and fast shutter speed).
- Handle tricky exposures such as contre-jour or high/low key situations easily.
- Effortlessly use hyperfocal distance techniques when required.
- Able to post process to reflect a personal style.
- Know how to use appropriate and wide-ranging composition skills to create a previsualised photograph.
- Know how perceived depth of field changes with different focal lengths.
- Know own lenses inside out: minimum focus distances, angles of view, aperture ranges.
- See the light and use it as a composition element all to itself.
- Able to predict what will happen and be ready to fire the shutter without a second thought when the composition is ready.
- Have a recognisable style.

TRY THIS

Try something so far outside your experience and technical abilities that no one (including yourself) could expect you to get it right first time. Enjoy the feeling of not being an expert straight away. Macro or still life photography are good places to start if you've not tried them before.

Here's how to do this. Find a photograph you want to take but currently don't think you could. Make a list of all the things you need to learn or practice in order to take this photograph. Research online, ask your friends and ask people at your photography club. Work through your list in the full knowledge that you will not get it first time, that you'll have to keep researching and practicing. Know that whatever progress you make, in whatever direction – yes, sometimes we go backwards – at least you didn't just stay in the same place waiting for something to happen.

4. FEAR OF FAILURE

Hopefully you now have realistic expectations about what you can achieve today with your camera, but you haven't lost the high expectations about what you might achieve in the future. Don't let the previous section stop you from dreaming big.

Once you start to dream big and imagine what you might accomplish, the fear of failure often pops its head up and stops you from even taking the next step. Because if you don't take the next step there's no way you can fail, right?

Acknowledging that you are afraid to fail is a good start. Try reframing the measure of your success. You might dream of winning *Wildlife Photographer of the Year* but make sure you view every mistake and failure on your journey towards that goal as a success simply because you are progressing.

TRY THIS

Dream big for a moment. If you couldn't fail, what would you like to achieve with your camera? An exhibition? A competition win? Going professional? Perhaps a line of greetings cards? Write that goal in the final box below. As you work towards it, write down evidence of each time you try something and it doesn't work first time. Buy a pack of gold stars and stick one in each time you fail like this. If you don't have stars draw yourself a smiley face or give yourself "10/10".

5. FEAR OF THE UNKNOWN

What we know is safe. We have an instinctive, primal fear of anything that is outside our known boundaries because it might kill us. When you try to venture outside what is known, even in abstract areas such as creativity, your subconscious will be digging its heels in to make you stay at home, to do what you know works. It doesn't want you rocking the boat.

To live a more creative life you have to walk beyond what you can see from where you are now. You have to take a step into the unexplored. Who knows what is out there? The only certain thing is that it will be different from where you are now.

Don't forget that creativity *needs* uncertainty to flourish. Without uncertainty you will just reproduce the same things you can already do. To be creative you need to practice experiencing and accepting the discomfort associated with venturing into the unknown. Remember to be present, enjoy the moment you are in rather than worrying about the unknown outcome.

The good news is that if you take steps to overcome your fear of the unknown in *any* situation, not just creative ones, the benefits will spill over into all areas of your life.

When have you ever overcome a fear of the unknown?

TRY THIS

1. What are the physical symptoms you notice when you think about trying something new with an uncertain outcome? Butterflies in the stomach? Increased heart rate? These are the same symptoms that we experience when we are excited – think about the night before your birthday when you were a child. Tell yourself you are not afraid, you are merely excited about what might happen and curious about the outcome.

2. Start with unknowns that have small consequences. Try reading a book by an unknown author or enrolling in a free online course in a subject you know nothing about. The worst that can happen is that you have wasted some time.

3. Build up to actions with bigger outcomes: for example, the next time you are in a new place for any reason set aside an hour to explore without a map. (Note: don't do this in wilderness areas or high crime districts).

4. When you are ready, jump in and try something with your camera where you don't know what will happen. Maybe you want to try developing your style, put your portfolio up for review, commit to holding an exhibition or invest time and money in a photography trip. Keep your mind open and stay curious rather than fearful.

6. FEAR OF THE BLANK CANVAS

I think there are two aspects to fear of the blank canvas, and they are at opposite ends of the creativity spectrum. The first is not knowing where to start, a kind of paralysis stemming from not having a single idea. The other is a paralysis caused by having too many ideas and not knowing which one to pick: a case of fear of missing out (FOMO): by creating "A" you necessarily don't create "B"and "C".

TRY THIS

If you have no ideas

There are a few methods of kick-starting your brain and turning on the creative tap.

1. Pick up your camera and start shooting. It doesn't matter what or where or how. Photograph the table you're sitting at, the bench you're waiting on, the kettle you're staring at. Keep shooting for half an hour. You might get nothing, but you might find the physical act of working with your camera reminds your neurons they are supposed to fire up new ideas.

2. Pick up a book, a newspaper or a magazine. Or open a web page. Count to the fifteenth word on any page and use that word, whatever it is, to prompt your next photograph.

3. Collect a colour. Spend the next day or the next week only shooting red things or blue things. This will train your brain to pay attention and seek out photography opportunities in unlikely places. You'll be surprised how many red or blue things you start to notice.

4. Focus on the process of creation rather than the final image. Resolve to compose carefully, examine the light and try different settings.

5. Imagine it's your friend who is having the problem getting started. What advice would you give them?

6. What displacement activities are you coming up with to delay starting? Once you recognise them as your subconscious sabotaging your progress it's easier to address them head on. I often find myself tidying my study, cleaning my sensor, doing the laundry or researching "one more inspiring photographer" before I think I am ready to start.

7. Play a mind-game: if you could go anywhere in the world with any gear at all, where would you go and what would you photograph? Write it down here:

Why do you think you want to go there and why did you pick those things to shoot? How can you adapt those preferences to a closer-to-home shoot?

If you have too many ideas
Just pick one. One idea given expression is better than six ideas that stay in your head.

7. FEAR OF BEING VULNERABLE

This section and the next were both first published in my online course, Mindful Photography. If this more thoughtful approach to photography is one that appeals you can find out more about this course at emmadavies.photo/courses.

As soon as you start to create, to put your work out there, to take risks, to try something different, you make yourself vulnerable; vulnerable to criticism, to mockery. Your rational brain will probably try to protect you from criticism by telling you not to create – "Stay safe, do the same thing that worked last time, just make things that people already like." That's fine, and you can spend your whole photography life on a comfortable plateau making things you like, staying safe, never showing work that people might not appreciate and never risking ridicule.

But if you want to make progress, find another side of yourself, create something more unique, actually get your art out into the world – then you'll need to take a risk and make yourself vulnerable.

I don't have any quick fixes for the fear of vulnerability. You can't make the feeling of vulnerability just go away and I don't think that should be your aim. You can become accepting of it though, recognise it as emotional progress. You can protect yourself from unnecessary vulnerability by choosing who you show your work to, and who you accept criticism from – choose people who are walking your walk not people who just watch you from the sidelines.

When you do pluck up the courage to show your work to someone you respect, are you ready to accept what they say? How do you respond to criticism? Imagine you have put an image you are proud of into a competition. It is judged anonymously. You don't do as well as you hoped. What's your reaction to the feedback? Do you get defensive? Blame the judge for not understanding your shot or for not being experienced enough? Or give up – "Well, that was my best shot so I'm clearly not good enough."

Be on the alert for these types of denial. There is always a grain of truth in feedback. You need to steel yourself to accept it graciously and gratefully. A fresh pair of eyes looking at your shot and giving you ideas for improvement is a gift, not something to be feared.

TRY THIS

Ask for a critique from someone whose advice you can trust. It should be someone who will not be jealous of your success or hold back for fear of hurting your feelings. Resolve to accept every comment without trying to justify what you did.

8. FEAR OF SUCCESS

Some people, consciously or not, fear success. It's often not the success itself that is the problem, but the things that might come with it. This fear is best broken down into parts:

- Fear of change.
- Fear of what people will say.
- Fear of selling out.
- Fear of other people's expectations once you've had a success.
- Fear of attention.
- Fear of seeming ambitious or greedy.
- Fear of becoming a different person.

If you find yourself struggling to get started with a big project, or not wanting to aim high, or starting but not finishing – it might be that you are a little afraid of what might happen if you succeed in your goal. Take some time to examine which part of the threat of success might be holding you back. Think about what the worst that could happen is. Think about the best that could happen. Which weighs more heavily with you – the fear of success, or the regret you might feel for not trying?

Success for you could be anything from finally taking your camera off auto (what if you're the only one in your group who can do it – will everyone see you differently?), to winning a photo competition (what next? – could you do it again?), or becoming a professional (is it wrong to take money for doing something you love?).

TRY THIS

Not everyone will struggle with success but if you do, find someone you trust to talk it through with. Or be that friend to yourself: write out the underlying reasons for your hesitations, and then write back to yourself as if you were writing to a friend, with advice.

Underlying reasons for hesitations:

Reply as a friend:

This has been a hard chapter. You don't need to address all your fears at once, and maybe some of them don't apply to you. Take a moment to rank the fears covered in this chapter in order of which apply most strongly to you. List the one you identify with most as number 1 and the one you identify with least as number 8. Then concentrate your efforts on the higher numbered fears.

The fears were:

- What's the point?
- It's hard work
- Fear of expectations
- Fear of failure
- Fear of the unknown
- Fear of the blank canvas
- Fear of being vulnerable
- Fear of success

1.

2.

3.

4

5.

6.

7.

8.

CHAPTER 8

The photography creative process

This chapter has seven different projects to kick-start your creativity. Most will take a little longer than the exercises so far. Take your time, pay attention to your thoughts and give each project your best shot.

LOST YOUR PHOJO?

Photographers don't lose their mojo, they lose their phojo. That feeling when you can't bear to pick up your camera, have no ideas of what to shoot or are stuck in a negative spiral of "It's all been done before so what's the point?"

TRY THIS

Here are a few tried-and-tested things to try when you're stuck:

- Take a complete break: no photographs at all, not even on your phone, for a whole week.
- Copy another photograph in as much detail as you can, one you love or one that intrigues you – the process of copying the work of the masters has a long history in art.
- Show up every day – commit to taking a daily photo for thirty days (use the tracker in Chapter 5 "Keep the good habits" if you skipped it first time around).
- Find (or create) a community to give you accountability.
- Do the "Fifty with fifty" challenge: you can take no other photographs until you have taken fifty consecutive images with a standard 50mm lens (or equivalent cropped frame focal length).
- Get out into nature if you can. For as yet unknown reasons, being in the great outdoors boosts creativity.

BIG PICTURE OR DETAIL?

In life generally where do you feel you sit on a scale that reads from "free-and-easy big-picture" to "you can't have too many details"?

Big picture **All the detail**

Is this the same for your photography and other creative output? Do you prefer a more abstract, impressionistic style or a very sharp, very detailed shot?

TRY THIS

There's no correct place to be on this scale in life or in art but most of us prefer one style over the other. Take this opportunity to really indulge your preferred approach for one project but also try to experience the other approach properly – give it the attention it deserves, don't discount it out of hand. If you don't have a preferred style then enjoy taking both approaches to your work.

If you prefer detailed, precise pieces then trying a very loose, abstract style will let your brain make new connections and feedback new ideas to your more controlled way of working. Conversely if you prefer a more relaxed way of working, focussing on the detail for a while will give you an opportunity to see how working in a more structured way affects your creativity.

Big picture

The sky is going to be your subject.

- Sketch the sky first: no erasing is permitted so use a permanent marker. Go for impression over detail.

- Next, complete a piece of writing in the space below: describe the sky with a stream of consciousness, unedited, loose. Write anything that comes to mind. Don't edit these ideas.

- Lastly, get your camera out and create one or more unfinished, messy, bold, experimental shots of the sky.

Stick in photo

Stick in photo

Detail

The subject will be something small and intricate that doesn't move so you can study it: a flower, a coin, a leaf, a small vegetable or a pencil.

- Draw the object first with as much detail as you can. Take care and make as many corrections as you want to:

- Complete a piece of writing: describe the thing as perfectly as you can with no wasted words and use only one sentence. Edit as much as you need to:

- Create one perfect photograph. Have as many trial runs as you need.

Stick in photo

COLLABORATE

What is your abiding memory of doing group projects at school or at work? Perhaps one person often ended up taking charge and making all the decisions, and maybe another person did most of the work. The rest of the group might have found they could keep a low profile and not need to get involved. This is not how creative collaboration should work. If you have bad memories of group work please humour me and keep an open mind for this section.

Good collaborations are truly "gestalt": the whole is bigger than the sum of the parts. This means the creative output from the group is better (more creative, more prolific and more original) than any single member could have achieved on their own.

If you approach a collaboration with an open mind you will be willing to look at what other people produce and be ready to take inspiration from that. Equally you will be willing to share your own ideas freely without worrying that they will be stolen. Everybody involved in a good collaboration recognises that success is measured by the output of the group as a whole rather than by any one member.

Think back to any group project you have ever done. What worked well and what didn't?

TRY THIS

Work as part of a collaboration to expand your comfort zone, expose yourself to unexpected ideas and to share your own ideas without reserve.

1. Photo to-and-fro

Find one friend to do this with. You take a photo and send it to them. They then take a photo inspired by yours and send that photo back to you. You do the same, and so on for as long as you can keep going.

2. Illustrate some writing

Do you know an author, a poet, someone writing a memoir or a recipe book? Very simply they send you their pieces of writing as they are completed and you take photos to illustrate. If the writer is up for a reverse-collaboration you can also send them photos you have taken as inspiration for their writing.

3. Joint exhibition

Get together with four to six other photographers and commit to putting on an exhibition together.

4. Model

This works well in small groups of two or three photographers. Each person takes their turn at modelling for the other photographer/s to give an unthreatening place for everyone to improve their portrait photography.

5. Start a collective

"Collective" is just an ambitious word for "group", but it does give your project a bit of gravitas. You'll need a theme. It might be simply taking photographs near where you live, or of a particular subject matter, or you might want to raise awareness of a social injustice. Start by inviting just one other photographer to collaborate. Have a place where you share your work – it might be a Facebook group, an Instagram hashtag or a joint website. Each of you can invite one further photographer to join, and each of them can do the same. Put a limit on the total number (maybe ten or so), after which someone has to leave before another person can join.

THE PLATEAU

When you learn photography – both the technical and creative aspects – you'll find you make a lot of progress very quickly. Much like a toddler learns to read, draw, eat by themselves, make friends and get on a swing all in the space of a week, so the new photographer discovers blurred backgrounds, the rule of thirds, how to use colour and freeze the action in a short space of time. Beginners often arrive quickly at the intermediate-level plateau and enjoy the view. On this plateau you can take good photos, people say nice things about them and you are happy with your work.

But getting off the plateau and onto the next peak is harder work than the first part of your journey. There is no low hanging fruit and there are no easy wins. You need to admit your good photos could be better, that there are things you don't know how to improve and that people might not like your work as you venture into the unfamiliar.

You might also find that you have lost what makes your photographs uniquely yours as you master aperture and shutter speeds, battle with a tripod and take full control over the light. Where is the spontaneity and fun? To use the toddler analogy again – once they go to school and have to hold a pencil correctly, only colour within the lines and write about what the teacher dictates, the child's own style will gradually be lost.

You need to watch out for the "easy" trap. It's easy always to shoot on your favourite aperture or frame your shots the same way. It's easy to shoot what you know – flowers, family, macro or landscape. Subconsciously you probably feel like you've done enough hard work on your first steep learning curve so you'll need to make an extra effort to admit there is still progress to make.

As you move off the intermediate plateau be ready. Your shots will get worse before they get better. They might not be as popular on Instagram. You'll almost certainly start to do worse in your camera club competitions. You might be unsure of what you are doing and where you are going. You've left the safety of driving on auto-pilot and you're responsible for your every move, with both the risks and the rewards (personal satisfaction) that will result.

TRY THIS

Where are you on this journey? Mark with an "X" where you are at the moment:

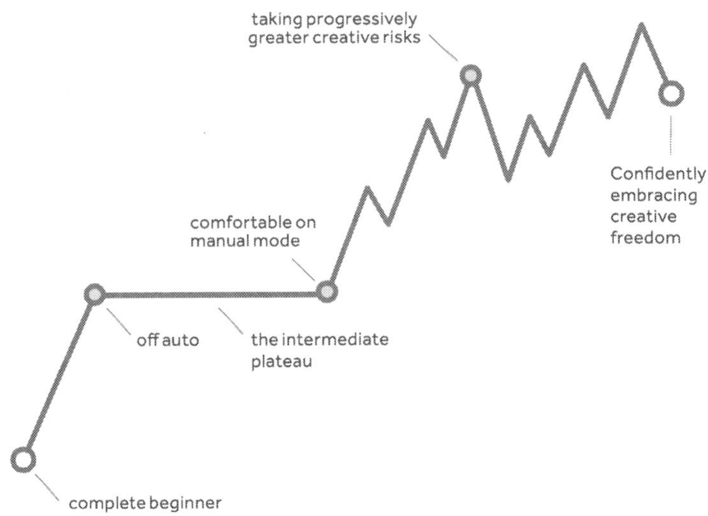

CONSTRAINTS

Creative thought does not thrive without constraints. Being told to "go off and take some photographs", "write about anything" or "draw whatever you like" means your brain has nothing to latch on to and nowhere to start.

You will find you are far more creative if there are constraints in place, even artificial ones that you make up: a time limit, a restricted subject matter or a specific end-use.

The pandemic lockdown has demonstrated this concept: limit the space you can move in and watch your brain be forced to get creative with ideas. Landscape photographers have started doing kitchen still lifes, wedding photographers have become daily-life photojournalists and travel photographers have become backyard macro photographers.

Instead of having the freedom to create a preconceived image whether in the studio or by travelling to a particular place at a particular time, we were forced to fall back on the bare bones of photography – creating images with what we had at home. After initial irritation with cancelled plans, resistance to the new limits and – dare I say it – a bit of sulking, we gradually discovered that if you have a camera you not only can you make photographs anywhere, you can actually enjoy it.

Distancing ourselves from the familiar, being forced to think differently – it was an unexpected opportunity. It was also global - so there was no fear of missing out.

Think about your creative life so far. Describe a project that had constraints: what were they and how did you react to them? Did someone else impose them or did you set the boundaries?

TRY THIS

I'm writing this in July 2020 when the virus is still with us but lockdown is lifting gradually. If you are reading this when lockdown is still fresh in your memory and your experience of the pandemic is still too raw you may prefer to do some of the other exercises first. If not, try some of these location-constrained creative projects I embarked on during lockdown:

- Document your neighbourhood on foot. Revisit the same place every day. I did this for sixty days during March and April 2020, photographing exactly the same forty-five minute walk through my local woods.
- Make the ordinary extraordinary. What can you do with a fork, a glass or a lemon?
- Shadows: make the shadow the subject.
- Revisit your archives: go back and re-edit some of your old shots.

Being constrained by end-use is also a good way to fire up your creativity by shutting down other options:

- Create a collection of images suitable for a range of greetings cards. Go one step further and actually get them printed.
- Tell a story with your camera, as if you are illustrating a piece for the Sunday papers. Document a local event, describe the history of somewhere interesting or create a travel guide.
- Consider working towards a qualification and start to get a suitable portfolio together.
- Enter a competition. *A Year With My Camera* student Anne MacIntyre tried the "take lots of photos of the same subject" creativity constraints exercise from my course. Her shot of two cosmos flowers won the black and white category of *International Garden Photographer of the Year.*

CONSISTENCY

Having the discipline to develop a style is a good skill to learn as a creative, even if you only keep that style for one particular project.

TRY THIS

Create a set of twelve photos that are linked in some way but not necessarily all shot on the same day. Imagine them displayed on a wall – they should look like they belong together. They could be of the same or similar subject (e.g. flowers or birds), using the same technique (e.g. long exposure water shots) or you could use the same post processing style. This exercise will help you focus your attention as you look for a common theme and then maintain it throughout the series.

Some ideas:

- Shots taken along a favourite walk.
- Self-portraits or pet portraits.
- Imagine you are illustrating a tourist guide to the place you live.
- Food photography: illustrate a favourite recipe or try still life with food.
- Macro flowers.

PERSONAL PROJECT

You've worked through the individual creativity exercises in this workbook, you've got a list of ideas, you've imposed some constraints and you're ready to work on a personal photography project.

TRY THIS

A personal project should be something that comes from the heart, something that allows your creative voice to be heard. It could be a single print or a series, a postcard or a portfolio, a slideshow or an album. Use the space opposite to write down some ideas.

Take your time. Don't rush this.
What are you curious about? What do you daydream about? Take pictures that you *love*.

Banish the guilt and make time for this project. If you have children or other demands on your time it can be difficult to find space for a personal project. But we make time for the things that are important to us. So if this is important to you embrace the time you set aside to do it without guilt.

You don't need to show the shots to anyone. In fact if you are on Instagram or any other social media platform consider **not** sharing your shots: that way you won't be influenced to create what you think will do well rather than listening to what is coming from inside. If you hear the word "should" in your head, think again. For example, if you think to yourself "I should take macro photographs because I have a macro lens."; no. Take macro photographs only if you **want to** for this project.

Enjoy the preparation stage, but don't wait to have the perfect idea completely planned out before you start. Start before you're ready and let your brain make new connections as you go. It's OK to change direction once you've started.

1. **Write down all the ideas you've got:**

2. **Circle your favourite three ideas.**

3. Expand on each of those three ideas.
Create a mind map – write the idea in the centre of the page and then write down ideas as they come to you branching out of the central idea.

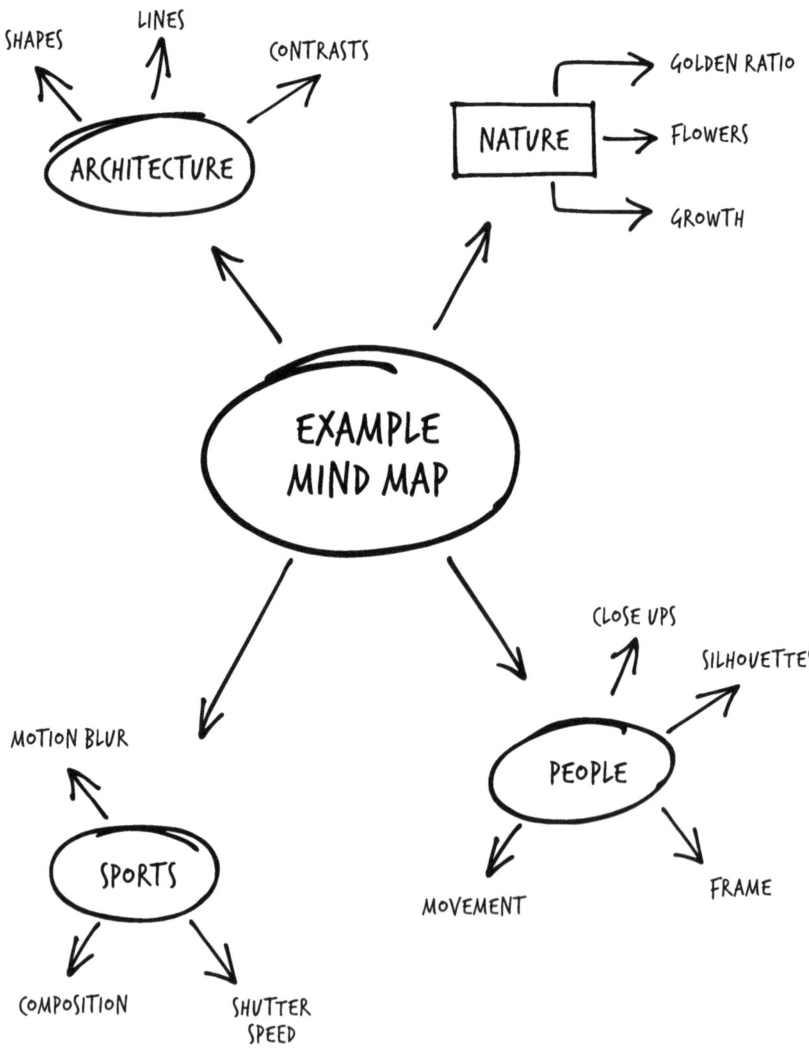

Example mind map

Mind map 1

Mind map 2

Mind map 3

4. Pick one idea.

Choose your favourite somehow. Stick a pin in one or go with your intuition – it doesn't matter. The other ideas will still be here when you've finished.

What's your one idea?

5. Reviewing

This part of the output stage is essential. You need to be in a good place to critique your own work objectively so work on your self-esteem and remember you are critiquing the photograph not the photographer.

When you have a body of photographs that are the rough first draft of your project there are a few extra steps you need to take:

- Edit in the traditional sense (not in the post-processing sense). You are the gatekeeper between yourself as photographer and your audience. Check your photographs make sense as a group and discard shots that are too similar or don't add anything. Every image needs to earn its place.
- Critique your shots kindly but firmly. Imagine you are offering advice to a friend who really wants to improve.
- Leave them be for at least a few days and then repeat. You will come back to them with fresh eyes to re-edit and re-evaluate.
- Get someone else to look at them if you can. Someone you trust, someone whose opinion you respect and someone who understands what you are trying to do.

Going public

Will you share your creative output with the wider world or will you keep it private?

Reasons to share

1. Sharing your work keeps you focussed and helps you create your best work. If you know other people are going to see your work you'll be less inclined to cut corners.
2. Sharing means you have to finish your project. It is often easy to do the first eighty percent of any project, but the last twenty percent is extremely difficult, motivationally.
3. People might like it, and they might tell you that. It's a nice feeling.
4. You'll get an immense sense of satisfaction from starting, finishing and sharing something.
5. If you want to sell your work, you'll be raising your profile by sharing it regularly.

Reasons not to share

1. If you're only doing this for external validation, think about your motivations. Will your project seem less valuable if nobody sees it? Or if nobody likes it?
2. Can you accept the fact that not everybody will like it? If it will set you back too much mentally or creatively when somebody tells you they don't like it, then share carefully and with a smaller audience.
3. It can be expensive if you want to hold an exhibition in terms of printing, framing and renting space. Online sharing is an alternative.

CHAPTER 9

About me now

Have I had fun?

	1	2	3	4	5	6	7	8	9	10	
No	○	○	○	○	○	○	○	○	○	○	Yes

Will I keep having fun?

	1	2	3	4	5	6	7	8	9	10	
No	○	○	○	○	○	○	○	○	○	○	Yes

Am I creative?

	1	2	3	4	5	6	7	8	9	10	
No	○	○	○	○	○	○	○	○	○	○	Yes

Do I know how to get started with a new project?

	1	2	3	4	5	6	7	8	9	10	
No	○	○	○	○	○	○	○	○	○	○	Yes

What am I afraid of now when I pick up my camera?

Currently, is my life with my camera joyful, spontaneous, audacious, instinctive and liberated?

It is:

not joyful									joyful
1	2	3	4	5	6	7	8	9	10
○	○	○	○	○	○	○	○	○	○

not spontaneous									spontaneous
1	2	3	4	5	6	7	8	9	10
○	○	○	○	○	○	○	○	○	○

not audacious									audacious
1	2	3	4	5	6	7	8	9	10
○	○	○	○	○	○	○	○	○	○

not instinctive									instinctive
1	2	3	4	5	6	7	8	9	10
○	○	○	○	○	○	○	○	○	○

not liberated									liberated
1	2	3	4	5	6	7	8	9	10
○	○	○	○	○	○	○	○	○	○

What will I do to move the needle in the right direction?

Notes

NOTES

Acknowledgements

Jez and Hayley from Wildcat Creative turned my dry manuscript into this beautiful workbook and I can't thank them enough.

Caroline Goldsmith edited my words with skill and patience. The fact you can read this book without tripping over my inelegant sentences is down to her.

I have been inspired by many creative people, both academics and artists. For further reading please turn to:

Twyla Tharp: The Creative Habit

Philippa Stanton: The Conscious Creativity series

John S Couch: The Art of Creative Rebellion

Elizabeth Gilbert: Big Magic - Creative Living Beyond Fear

Design: Wildcat Creative
Editor: Caroline Goldsmith
Brand: Orangery Creative

Printed by Amazon Italia Logistica S.r.l.
Torrazza Piemonte (TO), Italy

16187440R00066